# SHOW ME
# HAPPY

To my grandson, Lucas, whose smile
inspired this book—K.M.A.

To Laura and all our kids—E.F.

Thank you to all the families who graciously gave their time
to be photographed for this book—K.M.A. and E.F.

Library of Congress Cataloging-in-Publication
Data is on file with the publisher.

Text copyright © 2015 by Kathryn Madeline Allen
Photographs copyright © 2015 Eric Futran
Published in 2015 by Albert Whitman & Company
ISBN 978-0-8075-7349-5
Printed in China.
10 9 8 7 6 5 4 3 2 1 HH 20 19 18 17 16 15 14

The design is by Jordan Kost.

For more information about Albert Whitman & Company,
visit our web site at www.albertwhitman.com.

# SHOW ME
# HAPPY

Kathryn Madeline Allen          photographs by Eric Futran

ALBERT WHITMAN & COMPANY
CHICAGO, ILLINOIS

Show me happy,

show me helping,

show me up,

show me down.

Show me holding,

show me giving,

show me hiding,

show me found.

Show me pushing,

show me pulling,

show me sharing when we play.

Show me NOISY,

show me quiet,

show me putting things away.

Show me little,

show me BIG,

show me one

and show me ten.

Now, with some kisses...

and some hugs...

let's show we're happy to be friends.